'Away an' Ask Yer Mother!'

Allan Morrison

ILLUSTRATED BY

www.vitalspark.co.uk

The Vital Spark is an imprint of
Neil Wilson Publishing Ltd
303 The Pentagon Centre
36 Washington Street
GLASGOW G3 8AZ

Tel: 0141-221-1117
Fax: 0141-221-5363
E-mail: info@nwp.co.uk
www.nwp.co.uk

© Allan Morrison, 2005

First published in June 2002
Reprinted March 2005
The author has asserted his moral right
under the Design, Patents and Copyright Act
1988 to be identified as the Author of this Work.

All illustrations © Rupert Besley, 2005
Reproduction of illustrations is strictly prohibited
without the express permission of the
artist and publisher.

A catalogue record for this book is
available from the British Library.

ISBN 1-903238-56-0

Typeset in Bodoni
Designed by Mark Blackadder

Printed and bound in Poland

Contents

Introduction		7
1	HIS FAVOURITE SAYINGS	12
2	HIS SILLY WEE SAYINGS	18
3	GAINING SUCCESS IN LIFE	30
4	WHEN WE WERE ANNOYING HIM	37
5	GROWING UP	45
6	BEING ASTUTE IN LIFE	48
7	WHEN HE HAD HAD A WEE DRAM!	53
8	STORIES AND POEMS ABOUT DADS	58

Introduction

SCOTTISH DADS

What's the best advice a father can give his children? IT'S HERE IN THIS BOOK.

In addition to saying 'Away an' ask yer mother', dads do actually provide advice themselves, that is when they are not busy doing something important, like reading a newspaper or preparing to visit their local. You see, dads are special, and of course, SCOTTISH DADS ARE EXTRA SPECIAL.

SO WHAT IS A SCOTTISH FATHER? Someone who is proud to be Scottish but who is even more proud of his family. Someone who wants to keep you from making the mistakes he made, but mostly lets you find your own way. Scottish Dads may like to think they're big and strong, but will hold you when you cry, shine with pride when you succeed, and still have faith in you if you fail.

Basically the archetypal Scottish Dad is a man who expects his offspring to be as good as he meant to be. You see, truthfully, there are some things he is not really good at: shopping, reading instruction books, and you may recall he didn't seem to win a lot of board games when you were small.

And as for Dad's advice, you may well ask where did fathers learn the things they told their sons and daughters not to do?

It is said that the first duty of a loving father is to

 Away an' Ask Yer Mother

listen. Then you in turn had to listen to this purveyor of wisdom with his *bons mots* advising us on character, happiness and success amongst other things, sentiments that will remain timeless.

And remember it's a tough job, for as you teach your children, so too you teach your children's children.

YES, FATHERHOOD PROVIDES ONE OF LIFE'S MOST CHALLENGING TASKS!

AUTHOR'S NOTES: I am indebted to the many people who kindly provided me with their father's sayings. Where necessary, a translation of a saying is given.

> WHEN GOD MADE SCOTTISH FATHERS,
> he made a larger frame for them than
> for Scottish mothers.

> 'Excuse me, God,' asked a wee angel.
> 'How are they going to manage to get down
> and play on the floor with their children?
> And another thing: they'll need to bend
> over to tuck their offspring into bed.'

> God smiled and said, 'Well you see,
> children need someone to look up to.'

> WHEN GOD MADE SCOTTISH FATHERS,
> he gave them brains larger than other fathers'.

Away an' Ask Yer Mother

'Excuse me, God,' asked the angel.
'Why the extra-sized brains?'

'So, my dear,' said the Holy One,
'they can earn pennies to keep their
little ones. Also, Scottish Fathers need to
be clever to invent lots of useful
things for my world.'

WHEN GOD MADE SCOTTISH FATHERS,
he gave them bonny legs and knees.

'Excuse me, God,' asked the wee angel.
'Why those nice legs and knees?'

'Just to encourage them to wear
their kilts, my dear!'

WHEN GOD MADE SCOTTISH FATHERS,
he gave them great big feet.

'Excuse me, God,' asked the angel.
'Do you honestly think that Scottish Fathers
will swing those hulking great feet out of bed
in the middle of a cold night, and go and look after a
bawling babe?

'Of course,' replied the Almighty.
'Anyway, they will want to show up that
lot of English sinners at the fitba!'

Away an' Ask Yer Mother

FATHERHOOD QUOTES

Scottish fathers are men who give away their daughters to other men who aren't nearly good enough, so they can have grandchildren who are smarter than everybody else's.
Anon

Being a Dad is just like shaving.
No matter how good you do it today, you still have to do it again tomorrow.
Anon

There are three rules to being a great father. Patience, patience, patience!
Anon

Father's advice is least heeded, when father's advice is most needed!
Anon

Fatherhood is something that teaches you loyalty, forbearance, self-restraint and forgiveness.
Anon

Fathers saying 'yes' to a child is like blowing up a balloon. They have to know when to stop.
Anon

It doesn't matter who your dad was, but it's vital you remember – he was your father!
Anon

Away an' Ask Yer Mother

Anyone can be a Dad, but it takes a
man to be a Father.
Anon

A Dad is a man who has photos in his wallet
where his money used to be.
Anon

One guid Scottish faither is worth
half-a-dozen 'o they teachers.
Anon

1. His Favourite Sayings

Away an' ask your mother!

Just wait till I get you home!

My faither used to tell me …

Everyone in this house is entitled to my opinion!

When I was your age …

Away an' Ask Yer Mother

No, no. It's no' a tear. It's just something in my eye.

Don't come it wi' me!

If it wisnae for the last minute, a lot of things would never get done in this house.

Don't be a 'has-been'. Be a 'will-be'.

If you don't have the time to do it right, when will you have the time to do it over?

You're jist like your mother ower again.

Och, problems are jist opportunities in overalls!

Some that has the least tae dree are loudest wi' 'wae's me.

Don't find fault, find a remedy.

You're a wee gem.

You're a wee stoater.

Away an' Ask Yer Mother

You're a wee smasher.

We'll see!

Facts are chiels that winna ding.
(Facts cannot be denied.)

He who hesitates is sometimes wise!

Ah, ye aw ma ain back teeth.
(Don't think I'm daft.)

Worry gives a wee thing a big shadow.

Secrets are only things you give
to others to keep for you.

A good fellow is a costly name.

Are you at it?

Away an' Ask Yer Mother

There's no right way to do the wrang thing.

They aw get a richt Hieland Welcome in this hoose.

It's only a wee dream you're having, don't be scared.

Right you. Aff tae blanket bay.

Come here an' ah'll kiss it better.

Their heid's no' sair that did that.
(Whoever did this is surely dead by now.)

Better lang little than soon nothing.

Lang foul, lang fair.

If you don't like it, ye can lump it!

The best laid schemes o' mice
and men gang aft agley.

Good enough is
no' good enough.

Half a tale is enough
for a wise man.

Ah picked it up wi' the
wan haun' as the coo
learned the flingin'.
(I'm self-taught.)

 Away an' Ask Yer Mother

Away an' Ask Yer Mother

A hired horse never tired.

Help ma boab!

Tam maun ride.
(I must be on my way. Taken from
Robert Burns, *Tam O, Shanter*.)

Ye'll need tae tak us as ye find us.

There are saner folks oot by.

Folks may doubt whit ye say, but they
always believe whit ye do.

It's ok wi' me if it's ok wi' yer mother.

**Children are natural mimics. They try
to act like their father in spite of all
their mother's best efforts to teach
them good manners.**
Anon

2. His Silly Wee Sayings

Every family has some sap!

Clean aff a chair an' sit doon.

Ma stomach thinks ma throat is cut.

The trouble with getting wiser is that you have to get older at the same time.

Failure follows the path of least resistance.

He's a plumber on his mother's side.

If you're too big for yer breeks, you're exposed in the end.

There's only one way to improve memory. Lend the family money.

Monday's a terrible way tae spend a seventh o' yer life.

Away an' Ask Yer Mother

It wid dae a blind man guid tae see it!

Are ye readin' that paper ye're sittin' oan?

Whit butter an' whisky cannae cure,
there's nae cure fur.

Away an' wauchle!

It's difficult choosin' between twa blin' coos.

Bear an' forbear.

If you think the Cooncil don't care, jist try
missin' a couple o' payments.

Life's like Rudolph the red-nosed reindeer.
If you're no' in front then the scenery never changes.

Away an' Ask Yer Mother

The difference between genius and stupidity
is that genius has its limits.

Yer as guid as ten men missing!

In twa days, the morra will be yesterday.

Ye need tae dae whit ye have tae dae, afore ye
can dae whit ye want tae dae!

It's nae use boiling cabbage the twice.

Ance awa, aye awa.

Ye know ken whit ah mean hen!

Away an' Ask Yer Mother

If it's tae be, it's up tae me!

Soup should be seen and not heard!

You remind me o' a toothache ah once had.

Keep yer heid an' yer feet warm an' the rest will come tae nae harm.

Away an' take a tummle tae yersel.

He who thinks by the inch and talks by the mile, deserves to be kicked by the foot!

When you get tae ma age ye'll understaun.

Away an' Ask Yer Mother

The older the fiddle the sweeter the tune.

That milk cam frae the coo's mooth.

It wisnae fur naething that the cat licked the stane.

Daring and doing beats worrying and waiting.

You certainly brighten up ma day. You never turn aff a light in this hoose!

If ye're born tae be hanged then ye'll no' be drowned.

If you think it's going well, you've aye forgotten something.

You've goat a heid on ye like a stair-heid!

Ah've freens in baith places. (I know people who have gone to Heaven and folks who have gone to Hell.)

Away an' Ask Yer Mother

Ilka-day braw maks a Sabbath-day daw.
(If you wear your best clothes everyday, then you'll
have nothing to wear on special occasions.)

A'm gaun tae see the engines.
(Used by fathers on Clyde steamers
before they headed for the bar.)

I think I'll jist take a wee
dauner doon the road.

If some folks would talk
only when they think,
they'd hear a pin drop.

Aw things hae an end,
but a loaf has twa.

What winna mak a
pot may mak a pot lid.

Och, lads wid be men!

The sun always shines
oan a Saturday.

Aye, if wishes were
horses then beggars
wad ride, and aw the
world be drooned
in pride.

Away an' Ask Yer Mother

Care wid kill a cat, and yet there's
nae living withoot it.

Edinburgh's big, but Biggar's bigger.

That's the best feather in yer wing.
(That's what you're best at.)

He who finds no fault in himself
needs a second opinion.

A rent's better than a darn.
(Don't cover up your mistakes.)

You'll go stony-broke if
you wait aroon the hoose waitin' for a break!

Ye'd be better copying McKissock's coo!
(You'd be far better listening
than talking all the time.)

Away an' Ask Yer Mother

Lithgow for wells,
Glasgow for bells, and
Falkirk for beans,
bairns and peas!

Unhappy fish get
unhappy worms.

Ca me whit ye like
but dinna ca me over!

If ye fell oot the windae
ye'd fa' up the way.

Aye, an' the funny wee
man wi' nae arms
wull catch a hare!

Flattery's the same as gum. Enjoy it,
but don't swallow it.

Aw things thrive but thrice.

You lot wid eat me oot o' hoose an' hame.

Content is nae bairn o' wealth.

The best gift's the present.

Away an' Ask Yer Mother

'Every man has his ain trade,'
said the farmer tae the bishop.

Away an' tummle
yer wilkies!

The sooner you fall behind, the more time
you have to catch up!

If God had wanted us tae touch oor toes,
he'd of stuck them oan oor knees.

It's as auld as the Moss o' Meigle.

Away an' tummle yer wilkies!

Away an' Ask Yer Mother

The burn wid lose its sound if God removed the rocks.
(You need challenges in life.)

If swimmin' wis easy, they'd ca' it fitba.

A mile o' Don's worth aw o' Dee, except
for salmon, stane and tree.

He who hesitates is probably right.

Away an' stick it up yer jowks!

Away an' bile yer can!

Away an' Ask Yer Mother

That's the end o' an' auld song.

Every man has his ain Bubbly-Jock!

Ye look like a bratie.

A favourable wind disnae blow forever.

Don't work up a head of steam until
you know what's cooking!

A guid tale is no' the waur o' being twice told.
(Good advice is worth being repeated.)

Naebuddy listens until you make a mistake.

Away an' Ask Yer Mother

It's no' aften ah'm wrang
but ah'm right again!

A guid steel is worth a penny.
(You only get what you pay for.)

Things turn out best for people who make the
best of the way things turn out.

It's as black as Dick's hatband,
an' tied roon nine times tae.
(It's never ending.)

You're too previous!

Never died a winter yet!

A horn spoon hauds nae poison.
(The meals in our house are
plain but healthy.)

Ah'm away tae break eggs wi' a stick.
(I've a lot to do today.)

A father's advice is like castor oil.
Easy to give, but awful to take.
Anon

3.
Gaining Success in Life

Aim for the moon even if you
only hit the lamppost.

Don't wait for success, go ahead without it.

If you don't believe in yourself
naebuddy else will.

Thought is action in rehearsal.

Ye cannae climb the ladder of success
wi' yer hands in yer pockets.

The guid calf is better than a calf
o' ony other kind.

The one who quits last … wins!

If you always do what you have always done,
then you'll always get what you have always got.

Greatness never came from not trying.

Honesty is a trail.
Once you get off it you're lost.

Away an' Ask Yer Mother

A hard beginning is a guid beginning.

Everybody gets knocked down.
Champs get back up.

Stick in at the school or ye'll end up
on sweer corner.

If you're in deep water keep
your mouth shut.

Success is how high you bounce
when you hit the bottom.

Away an' Ask Yer Mother

A bad wound may heal,
but a bad name will kill.

Ideas don't work till you do.

The man at the top of the mountain
didn't fall there!

Don't be afraid to give up good and go for great!

A layin' hen is better
than a standin' mill.

Ye cannae plough the field jist by
turnin' it ower in yer mind.

Away an' Ask Yer Mother

If you don't want anyone to know, don't do it.

Never be so skint that you cannot
afford to pay attention.

If you think you can't, you won't.
If you think you can, you will.

If black's yer apron, ye'll aye be washing it.
(If you get a bad name, you'll have
difficulty changing it.)

Before you are a 'has been', you have to
have been a 'something' to start with.

Away an' Ask Yer Mother

An excuse is a poor patch for the coat of failure.

Quitters never win and winners never quit!

Dare weel tae fare weel.
(You've sometimes got to be bold to get on in this life.)

Learn to tell the difference between
conscience and cold feet.

Good, better, best, never let it rest, till your
good is better, and your better's best!

Success comes in cans, not cannots.

It's better to try and fail, than fail to try.

Away an' Ask Yer Mother

If you're afraid to go too far,
you'll never go far enough.

It's nae use putting thatch on an empty barn.

Don't look where you fell, look where you slipped.

Potential means you haven't yet done your best!

If opportunity doesn't knock, build your own door.

Ye've a guid tongue in yer head, speir!
(When in doubt, ask)

**When the tough get going, the
tough get their faither.**
Anon

4.
When We Were Annoying Him

If ah take ma haun aff yer bum ye'll never smile again.

Ye're as wild as the heather!

Stop that shouting. The whole close will hear you.

Away an' pit yer heid in the jawbox.

Ah'm goannae lose the heid in a minute!

Ah dinnae lift ye afore ye fa'!

Yer as bold as wan o' they Lammermuir lions!
Note: There are no lions in the
Lammermuir Hills!

Have you taken the grumble-face?

I am sick an' tired o' the whole jing-bang lot of ye.

Less o' yer jaw an' mair o' yer legs!

Ok. Be bad. It'll save Santa a trip.

Away an' Ask Yer Mother

Well, I'll tell you why. It's for the same reason that
Aberdeen cats never drink cream.
(You're not going to be given the chance.)

A hantle cry murder, and are aye upmost.
(You're just like those folks who are always
shouting their heads off.)

Ye're a cheeky wee rascal!

You'll be laughin' water in a minute!
(You'll be crying soon.)

Will ye stoap yer cairryoan!

Excuses are like belly buttons - useless!

Ah've seen wiser eatin' grass.

Away an' Ask Yer Mother

I'll gae ye a Hawick Hug!
(I'll give you a squeeze around the middle.)

Don't make me stop this car!

Away an' shoo a goose!

Ah think ah goat ye in a lucky bag!

Hurry up! Ye're like Paddy's ghaist,
aye twa steps behind.

Dunnadaeit!

Away an' Ask Yer Mother

If ye gie a bairn his will, an' a
dug its fill, nane o' them will e'er dae weel.

Deil a fear o' me!
(Most certainly not!)

Yer herr's minginhinginanclinging!

Ye're as daft as a gate in a
field oan a windy day!

Away an' take a powder!

Away an' behave.
I'm fair puggled.

Away an' Ask Yer Mother

Maidens should be mild and meek,
quick to hear an' slow to speak!

Quiet you! Ah've been knockin'
ma pan in aw day!

Ah'll gie ye the back o' ma haun in a minute!

In a minute ah'll clatter ye wi' ma bunnet!

Maybe that's ower north for you!
(Maybe it's gone over your head.)

You lot will neither dance nor haud the candle.
(You're a right lazy bunch!)

You don't have to like it.
You just have to eat it!

Away an' Ask Yer Mother

Away an' shake yer lugs!

Because I said so!

Ah might have a guid job but ah'm
no' the heid bummer.

It's no' a matter of if,
it's a matter of when.

Nae chance!'

Away an' Ask Yer Mother

You jist open yer mooth an'
let yer belly rumble!

That's daft claver!

What should not be heard by wee ears,
should not be said by big mouths.

Them wha gae jumpin'
awa' aft come limpin' back.

Away an' Ask Yer Mother

Away you tae Loch Eleven!
(Apparently Loch Leven was sometimes
called 'Eleven', as it's approximately eleven
miles round, has eleven burns leading into it,
is surrounded by eleven hills, has eleven small
islands, has eleven kinds of fish in its waters,
and Mary Queen of Scots was imprisoned
in the Castle there for eleven months.)

Self praise is something you get for nothing.

If you had brains you'd be dangerous!

You're the mither o' mischief an' you're no'
bigger than a midge's wing.

Ah'm talkin' tae the shovel no' the dirt!

Waly, waly, bairns are bonny, ane's
enough and twa's ower mony!

Pick a windae. Ye're leavin'!

Have you goat the first seat oan the midden the day?
(Are you in a bad mood?)

**Faithers make their baby girls into
wee wifies, an' when they become
wifies they turn them back again.**
Anon

5. Growing Up

I want you back in this house no later than …

A dear ship lied lang in the harbour.
(Some people are too fussy.)

A fire that is out is evil to kindle.
(Don't pursue relationships with old flames.)

Character is what you stand for,
reputation is what you fall for.

Now you behave or you'll go to the bad fire.
(If you're bad you'll go to Hell.)

Work like you don't need the money;
love like you've never been jilted; and
dance like nobody's watching.

Now, be good! And if you can't be
good be careful. And if you can't be
careful, don't ca' it efter me!

Watch it! Temptation always gives
you a second chance.

A lass wi' mony wooers aft picks the worst.

Away an' Ask Yer Mother

Teenagers are only good at giving
you the benefit of their inexperience.

What time of night do you call this?

A man at five may be a fool at fifteen.

Nae fizzers noo!
(Don't tell me any lies.)

You've a tongue on ye that would clip clouts.

Bees wi' honey in their mooths
hae stings in their tails.

Away an' Ask Yer Mother

The only exercise you seem tae
get is pushin' yer luck!

Be aff wi' the auld love afore
ye're on wi' the new.

Guid Enough has goat a wife,
an' Far Better wants!

A hasty meeting, a hasty parting.

Listen, the world wis doin' jist
fine till you arrived!

Beauty doesnae mak a man's parritch.

Four an' twenty tailors widna
mak a man o' ye.

Watch out for them that are
fain and fey.

**A faither is neither an anchor tae hold
us back, nor a sail to take us there, but
a guiding light tae show us the way.**
Anon

6. Being Astute in Life

Dinnae waste a penny candle
looking for a bawbee.

A guid face needs nae band, an'
an ill face deserves nane!

A freen at court is worth a bob or
two in yer pocket.

Never give cherries to a pig
or advice to a fool.

Away an' Ask Yer Mother

Never take yourself down
to anyone else's level.

A wise man carries his cloak in fair weather,
an' a fool wants his in the rain.

There are thousands of folks oot there
happy tae separate you from your money.

You only eat an elephant in wee bites.

Away an' Ask Yer Mother

A lie is half way roon this country
afore the truth has its boots oan.

Aye keep something fur a sair leg.

Don't try to catch twa frogs wi' the one hand.

Opportunity knocks, but temptation jist
stands ootside the door an' whistles.

Mair than enough is ower muckle.

Carrying an umbrella's nae good if
your shoes are letting in.

Don't count the days; make the days count!

There are only three kinds of folks
in this life. Right-handed, left-handed
and underhanded!

Believe a' ye hear, an' ye'll eat a' ye see.

The one thing you can give
and keep is your word.

Never underestimate the power of human stupidity.

Don't shake the tree ower hard,
you never jist know whit might fall oot.

Away an' Ask Yer Mother

Away an' Ask Yer Mother

A troot in the pan is better
than a salmon in the Tay.

A thread will tie an honest man better
than a rope the rogue.

There are no doctors who are poor.
But there are poor doctors.

If ye dance in the dark ken wha ye tak by the haun.

Every shoe fits not every foot.

Gie ower when the play's good!

A wild goose ne'er reared a tame gosling!

Faithers can sometimes be like old oil lamps. Some are bright, some are not. Some smoke, some don't. And some tend to go out just when you need them.
Anon

7. When He Had a Wee Dram!

Abstinence should only be
practised in moderation.

A watched clock never boils!

Ye cannae beat a broken drum.

Aye, it's better tae cut a tale wi' a drink.

That's the baw up oan the slates!

Remember. A loaded gun beats four aces!

Oh, me, my, ma maw. The drink wis
good but my throat is raw.

Get yer bahookie aff ma chair.

Do one to others afore others do one to you.

Aye, by the time you've made it,
you've had it.

Me drink water! I'd be afraid it
might become habit forming.

Away an' Ask Yer Mother

Men do whit they want.
Boys do whit they can.

Had ye sic a shoe on ilka foot,
it wid mak you shackle.
(If you had my troubles you would
be unhappy too.)

Ah'm away tae ma scratcher,

Some folks are like bagpipes. There's nae
squawk oot them till they're fu'!

A man's nae use when his wife's a widow.

You've goat a face oan ye
like a constipated coo!

Away an' Ask Yer Mother

O' aw the meat in the world, the whisky
goes doon the best.

Water's killed mere folks than whisky.
Remember the flood.

Ah've a pedlar's drouth on me.
(I'm hungry.)

God is God, God is fair,
Tae some he gave brains,
Tae me - nae hair!

Ah'm no' a steady drinker, you know.
Ma hauns shake too much!

Every dog has its day, an' a bitch
taw afternoons.

Ah'm that happy ah could burst a poke!

Never drink whisky with water, and never
drink water without whisky.

That's weel awa', as the man said when
his wife swallowed her tongue.

Ah need a hair o' the dog
that bit me.

Away an' Ask Yer Mother

And the poem that he recited to justify his occasional 'wee refreshment':

The horse and mule live 30 years
And nothing know of wines and beers.
The goat and sheep at 20 die
And never of the whisky buy.
The cow drinks water by the ton
And at 18 is mostly done.
The dog at 15 stops being frisky
Without the taste of rum and whisky.
The cat in milk and water soaks
And then in 12 short years it croaks.
The modest, sober, bone-dry hen
Lays eggs for us and dies at 10.
Animals are strictly dry
They sinless live and quickly die,
But sinful, beerful, dramsoaked men,

Survive for three score years and ten.
And some of them, a very few,
Stay pickled till they're 92!

By the time a man realises that maybe his father was right, he usually has a son who thinks he's wrong.
Anon

8. Stories and Poems about Fathers

A wee girl was watching her dad as he cleaned his car.

'Dad, why are some of the hairs on your head turning white?'

Her father was hurrying to finish the task in hand, so he replied somewhat irritably, 'Well, every time you do something wrong and upset me, one of my hairs turns white.'

His daughter pondered over this for a minute and then asked, 'Dad, how come Grampa's hair is all white?'

*   *   *

Father's day is always a worrying time for Scottish Dads. It's the time when they go broke giving out money so their children can surprise them with presents they don't need.

*   *   *

Two wee girls were coming home from church.

'Do you believe all this stuff aboot a devil?' asked one.

'Don't be daft,' replied the other. 'It's jist like Santa, it's yer faither.'

Away an' Ask Yer Mother

WHAT IS A DAD?

A Dad is a person,
Who is loving and kind,
And often he knows
What you have on your mind.
He's someone who listens,
Suggests and defends,
A Dad can be one
Of your very best friends.
He's proud of your triumphs,
But when things go wrong,
A Dad can be patient
Helpful and strong.
In all that you do,
A Dad's love plays a part,
There'll always be a place
For him deep in your heart.
And each year that passes,
You're even more glad,
More grateful and proud
Just to call him YOUR DAD.

Author unknown

* * *

A Glasgow father was giving his son a lecture about lying.
   'When I was your age I didn't tell lies.'
   'So how old were you when you started Dad?'

Away an' Ask Yer Mother

I MUST FOLLOW YOU DAD.

Walk a wee bit slower, Dad,
Said the little child so small.
Ah'm following in your footsteps,
And I dinnae want tae fall.
Sometimes yer steps are awfu' fast,
Sometimes they're hard to see.
So walk a wee bit slower, Dad,
For you are leading me.

Someday when I'm all growed up,
You're what I want to be,
Then I may have a tiny bairn,
Who'll want to follow me.
And I would want to lead it right,
And know that I was true.
So, walk a wee bit slower, Dad,
For I must follow you.

Author unknown.

Away an' Ask Yer Mother

There are little eyes upon you, Dad,
And they're watching night and day.
There are little ears that quickly take in
Every word you say.
There are little hands all eager to do anything you do,
And a little child who's dreaming to do anything
    you do.
You're the little child's idol,
You're the wisest of the wise,
In their little minds no suspicions e'er arise.
They believe in you devoutly,
Remembering all you say and do,
They will say and do in your way,
When they're all growed up like you.

There's a wide-eyed little person,
Who believes you're always right,
And their eyes are always opened,
As they watch you day and night.
You are setting an example,
Every day in all you do,
To the little child who's waiting
To grow up to be like you.

Anon

Away an' Ask Yer Mother

Away an' Ask Yer Mother

One hundred years from now, it will not matter how much you had in the bank, the kind of house you lived in, or the make of the car you drove.

But the world may be a little better because you were important in the life of your child.

* * *

The 96 year-old man lived by himself in the attic of a Glasgow tenement. His son of 74 tried to get his father to move in with his wife and himself, but his father flatly refused, saying, 'I hate having a wee upstart like you telling me what to do!'

* * *

If children live with criticism, they learn to condemn.
If children live with hostility, they learn to fight.
If children live with ridicule, they learn to be shy.
If children live with shame, they learn to feel guilty.
If children live with tolerance, they learn to be patient.
If children live with encouragement, they learn confidence.
If children live with praise, they learn to appreciate.
If children live with fairness, they learn justice.
If children live with security, they learn to have faith.
If children live with approval, they learn to like themselves.
If children live with acceptance and friendship, they learn to love the world.

* * *

WHO WAS MY FATHER?

Noo, Son. It's time ah telt ye,
Yer a big lad efter a.
It's only fair ye know the truth
Ah trust it's no' a blaw.

Ye've been a guid son aw these years,
Aye helpful, guid and true,
Never givin' us oany cheek
We must give you due.

At school ye've worked so awful well,
As good as any wean.
Yer homework was done each night
Exams passed without o'er strain.

We've loved you since you were a babe,
You were a lovely chiel,
Aye smilin' through those shining eyes
Aye prompt fur every meal.

Ah thocht ah widnae tell ye
Until you were really old,
But, ah've thocht aboot it often,
An' ah've decided to be bold.

Before ah tell ye you must know,
Ah haven't loved ye less.
So steel yourself for the news,
Please do not get depressed.

Away an' Ask Yer Mother

So, Son, ah must tell you,
It may not be your wish.
But the truth ye have tae know
Yer faither's EN-GL-ISH!

Anon

The Aberdonian father observed one day that his wife was having a problem getting their baby off to sleep for its afternoon nap.

'Remember, dear,' he observed. 'The hand that rocks the cradle rules the world.'

'Well, why don't you take over the world for a few minutes while I nip down to the shops.'

* * *

A Paisley father gave his boy a lecture on how, when he was young, he was seen and not heard, was always well behaved and went to bed immediately he was asked to do so.

After he left the room, his wife was heard to observe, 'Listen, son, you will find that the first thing that goes as you grow old is your memory.'

* * *

A Glasgow teenager had his CD player blaring with the latest song from the Top Twenty.

'Bet you never heard anything like that when you were young, Dad!'

'Oh aye, ah did. Ah remember once a midden motor running into a truck full o' coos.'

* * *

Away an' Ask Yer Mother

THE NAME

You got it from your father,
It was all he had to give,
So it's yours to use and cherish
For as long as you may live.

If you lose the watch he gave you
It can always be replaced.
But a black mark on your name, son,
Can never be erased.

It was clean the day you took it,
And a worthy name to bear,
When he got it from his Dad,
There was no dishonour there.

So make sure you guard it wisely,
After all is said and done.
You'll be glad the name is spotless
When you give it to your son.

Author unknown.

* * *

It was bedtime and there was a violent thunderstorm overhead in Perth. The wee girl was frightened.

'Mummy, will you sleep with me tonight?'

The mother gave her daughter a reassuring hug. 'I can't do that, ma wee pet. I've got to sleep with Daddy.'

There was a long silence after which a small voice said, 'Sure he's a big sissy, Mummy.'

* * *

An Edinburgh father and his son fell out badly. The son ran away to London. His father went down each weekend to look for his son. Finally, in despair, the father put an advert in the *London Evening Standard*: 'Stewart, meet me at Nelson's Column in Trafalgar Square at 2.00 on Saturday. I love you. All is forgiven. Dad.'

At 2.00 on Saturday, a dozen Stewarts turned up looking for their fathers, including the one from Edinburgh.

* * *

When I was 3 years old, I said, 'My Daddy can do anything.'
When I was 5 years old, I said, 'My Daddy knows a lot of things.'
When I was 7 years old, I said 'My Daddy is better than your Daddy.'
When I was 9 years old, I said, 'Perhaps my Dad doesn't know absolutely everything.'
When I was 12 years old, I said, 'My Dad is a wee bit old fashioned.'
When I was 21 years old, I said, 'Don't listen to him! He lives in the past.
When I was 28 years old, I said, 'Maybe I should ask

Dad. He,s got a lot of experience.'

When I was 35 years old, I said, 'Before I do anything I must ask Dad.'

When I was 45 years old, I said, 'I wonder what Dad would have done?'

When I was 50 years old, I said, 'Too bad I didn't appreciate him more. I miss him.'

* * *

WHO WAS MY FATHER?

Someone who went away to work early each morning and came home tired but pleased to see us all. You could hear him coming up the close stairs each night, whistling away. He could open a jar of Co-operative jam when no one else could. He would carry the coal up to our flat from the cellar below.

If he cut himself shaving nobody worried because he was capable of sorting out anything. He took lots of photographs of us but hardly appeared in any of them. Football, an occasional pint, and his family gave him pleasure. He was always around to help, give advice and a wee hug before you went to bed.

We loved him. He loved us.

Now he is gone.

* * *

THE FINEST MAN I KNOW.

His shoulders are a wee bit bent,
His youthful force is somewhat spent,
But he's the finest man I know,
With heart of gold and hair like snow.
He's seldom cross and never mean,
Always good is what he's been.

I only hope I'll always be
Kind to him as he's been to me.
Sometimes he's tired and seems forlorn,
His happy face is lined and worn,
Yet he can smile when things are bad,
That's why I love my Scottish dad.

He doesn't ask the world for much,
Just comfort, friendliness, and such;
But from the things I've heard him say,
I know it's up to me to pay,
For all the deeds he's done for me
Since I sat happily on his knee.

Oh, not in pounds, shillings and pence,
That's not a father's recompense,
Nor does he want wealth and fame,
Just me bring honour to his name.

Anon

*   *   *

Away an' Ask Yer Mother

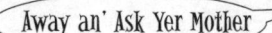

Be careful of the words you say, Dad,
Keep them short and sweet,
Because you'll never know from day to day,
Which ones you'll need to eat.

*   *   *

THE QUESTION!

She'd been so awfu' lucky,
Wi' 'Fastest Finger First',
The questions they'd just suited her,
Although she'd feared the worst.
Ok. So, she'd used her lifelines,
This lass fae a Scottish toon,
And then, 'Oh, Mammy, Daddy!'
Won hauf-a-million poon.

An' noo fur the million question,
It surely wid be tough.
She goat ready fur the big yin,
It wid be a stoater, right enough.
The audience hushed and tensed,
A' feared she heard the host.

Away an' Ask Yer Mother

HERE COMES THE QUESTION:
What do Fathers say most?

At the four options given,
She didnae glance or bother.
Sure she'd heard it aw her life,
'AWAY AN' ASK YER MOTHER!'

Anon